This Book Belongs To :

Emergency Contact

Name : _________________________ Relation : _______________

Address : ____

____

Work : _______________________ Cell : ____________________

Email : ______________________ Birthday : ________________

Note : ____

Name : _________________________ Relation : _______________

Address : ____

____

Work : _______________________ Cell : ____________________

Email : ______________________ Birthday : ________________

Note : ____

Name : _________________________ Relation : _______________

Address : ____

____

Work : _______________________ Cell : ____________________

Email : ______________________ Birthday : ________________

Note : ____

Page Index

Blank Page

Name: Date:

Website:

Password: PIN:

Email: Phone:

Security Question/Notes:

Name: Date:

Website:

Password: PIN:

Email: Phone:

Security Question/Notes:

Name: Date:

Website:

Password: PIN:

Email: Phone:

Security Question/Notes:

Name: Date:

Website:

Password: PIN:

Email: Phone:

Security Question/Notes:

Name: Date:

Website:

Password: PIN:

Email: Phone:

Security Question/Notes:

Name: Date:

Website:

Password: PIN:

Email: Phone:

Security Question/Notes:

Name: _______________________ Date: _______________

Website: _______________________________________

Password: ___________________________ PIN: _______

Email: _____________________ Phone: _____________

Security Question/Notes: ________________________

____

Name: _______________________ Date: _______________

Website: _______________________________________

Password: ___________________________ PIN: _______

Email: _____________________ Phone: _____________

Security Question/Notes: ________________________

____

Name: _______________________ Date: _______________

Website: _______________________________________

Password: ___________________________ PIN: _______

Email: _____________________ Phone: _____________

Security Question/Notes: ________________________

____

Name:

Date:

Website:

Password:

PIN:

Email:

Phone:

Security Question/Notes:

Name:

Date:

Website:

Password:

PIN:

Email:

Phone:

Security Question/Notes:

Name:

Date:

Website:

Password:

PIN:

Email:

Phone:

Security Question/Notes:

Name: Date:

Website:

Password: PIN:

Email: Phone:

Security Question/Notes:

Name: Date:

Website:

Password: PIN:

Email: Phone:

Security Question/Notes:

Name: Date:

Website:

Password: PIN:

Email: Phone:

Security Question/Notes:

Name: Date:

Website:

Password: PIN:

Email: Phone:

Security Question/Notes:

Name: Date:

Website:

Password: PIN:

Email: Phone:

Security Question/Notes:

Name: Date:

Website:

Password: PIN:

Email: Phone:

Security Question/Notes:

Name: .... Date: ....

Website: ....

Password: .... PIN: ....

Email: .... Phone: ....

Security Question/Notes: ....

....

Name: .... Date: ....

Website: ....

Password: .... PIN: ....

Email: .... Phone: ....

Security Question/Notes: ....

....

Name: .... Date: ....

Website: ....

Password: .... PIN: ....

Email: .... Phone: ....

Security Question/Notes: ....

....

Name: _______________________ Date: _______________________

Website: _______________________

Password: _______________________ PIN: _______________________

Email: _______________________ Phone: _______________________

Security Question/Notes: _______________________

____

Name: _______________________ Date: _______________________

Website: _______________________

Password: _______________________ PIN: _______________________

Email: _______________________ Phone: _______________________

Security Question/Notes: _______________________

____

Name: _______________________ Date: _______________________

Website: _______________________

Password: _______________________ PIN: _______________________

Email: _______________________ Phone: _______________________

Security Question/Notes: _______________________

____

Name: .... Date: ....

Website: ....

Password: .... PIN: ....

Email: .... Phone: ....

Security Question/Notes: ....

....

Name: .... Date: ....

Website: ....

Password: .... PIN: ....

Email: .... Phone: ....

Security Question/Notes: ....

....

Name: .... Date: ....

Website: ....

Password: .... PIN: ....

Email: .... Phone: ....

Security Question/Notes: ....

....

Name: _______________________ Date: _______________

Website: _______________________________________

Password: _____________________ PIN: ___________

Email: _____________________ Phone: ___________

Security Question/Notes: ________________________

____

Name: _______________________ Date: _______________

Website: _______________________________________

Password: _____________________ PIN: ___________

Email: _____________________ Phone: ___________

Security Question/Notes: ________________________

____

Name: _______________________ Date: _______________

Website: _______________________________________

Password: _____________________ PIN: ___________

Email: _____________________ Phone: ___________

Security Question/Notes: ________________________

____

Name: .... Date: ....

Website: ....

Password: .... PIN: ....

Email: .... Phone: ....

Security Question/Notes: ....

....

Name: .... Date: ....

Website: ....

Password: .... PIN: ....

Email: .... Phone: ....

Security Question/Notes: ....

....

Name: .... Date: ....

Website: ....

Password: .... PIN: ....

Email: .... Phone: ....

Security Question/Notes: ....

....

Name: ___________________________ Date: ___________

Website: ____

Password: ____________________________ PIN: _______

Email: ________________________ Phone: ___________

Security Question/Notes: _________________________

____

Name: ___________________________ Date: ___________

Website: ____

Password: ____________________________ PIN: _______

Email: ________________________ Phone: ___________

Security Question/Notes: _________________________

____

Name: ___________________________ Date: ___________

Website: ____

Password: ____________________________ PIN: _______

Email: ________________________ Phone: ___________

Security Question/Notes: _________________________

____

Name: Date:

Website:

Password: PIN:

Email: Phone:

Security Question/Notes:

Name: Date:

Website:

Password: PIN:

Email: Phone:

Security Question/Notes:

Name: Date:

Website:

Password: PIN:

Email: Phone:

Security Question/Notes:

Name: ___________________________ Date: ___________

Website: ____

Password: _______________________ PIN: ___________

Email: _________________________ Phone: __________

Security Question/Notes: _________________________

____

Name: ___________________________ Date: ___________

Website: ____

Password: _______________________ PIN: ___________

Email: _________________________ Phone: __________

Security Question/Notes: _________________________

____

Name: ___________________________ Date: ___________

Website: ____

Password: _______________________ PIN: ___________

Email: _________________________ Phone: __________

Security Question/Notes: _________________________

____

Name: Date:

Website:

Password: PIN:

Email: Phone:

Security Question/Notes:

Name: Date:

Website:

Password: PIN:

Email: Phone:

Security Question/Notes:

Name: Date:

Website:

Password: PIN:

Email: Phone:

Security Question/Notes:

Name: Date:

Website:

Password: PIN:

Email: Phone:

Security Question/Notes:

Name: Date:

Website:

Password: PIN:

Email: Phone:

Security Question/Notes:

Name: Date:

Website:

Password: PIN:

Email: Phone:

Security Question/Notes:

Name: Date:

Website:

Password: PIN:

Email: Phone:

Security Question/Notes:

Name: Date:

Website:

Password: PIN:

Email: Phone:

Security Question/Notes:

Name: Date:

Website:

Password: PIN:

Email: Phone:

Security Question/Notes:

Name: _______________________ Date: _______

Website: _______________________

Password: _______________________ PIN: _______

Email: _______________________ Phone: _______

Security Question/Notes: _______________________

____

Name: _______________________ Date: _______

Website: _______________________

Password: _______________________ PIN: _______

Email: _______________________ Phone: _______

Security Question/Notes: _______________________

____

Name: _______________________ Date: _______

Website: _______________________

Password: _______________________ PIN: _______

Email: _______________________ Phone: _______

Security Question/Notes: _______________________

____

Name: Date:

Website:

Password: PIN:

Email: Phone:

Security Question/Notes:

Name: Date:

Website:

Password: PIN:

Email: Phone:

Security Question/Notes:

Name: Date:

Website:

Password: PIN:

Email: Phone:

Security Question/Notes:

Name: Date:

Website:

Password: PIN:

Email: Phone:

Security Question/Notes:

Name: Date:

Website:

Password: PIN:

Email: Phone:

Security Question/Notes:

Name: Date:

Website:

Password: PIN:

Email: Phone:

Security Question/Notes:

Name: ____________________________ Date: ____________________

Website: ____

Password: ________________________ PIN: ____________________

Email: ___________________________ Phone: __________________

Security Question/Notes: ____________________________________

____

Name: ____________________________ Date: ____________________

Website: ____

Password: ________________________ PIN: ____________________

Email: ___________________________ Phone: __________________

Security Question/Notes: ____________________________________

____

Name: ____________________________ Date: ____________________

Website: ____

Password: ________________________ PIN: ____________________

Email: ___________________________ Phone: __________________

Security Question/Notes: ____________________________________

____

Name: Date:

Website:

Password: PIN:

Email: Phone:

Security Question/Notes:

Name: Date:

Website:

Password: PIN:

Email: Phone:

Security Question/Notes:

Name: Date:

Website:

Password: PIN:

Email: Phone:

Security Question/Notes:

Name: Date:

Website:

Password: PIN:

Email: Phone:

Security Question/Notes:

Name: Date:

Website:

Password: PIN:

Email: Phone:

Security Question/Notes:

Name: Date:

Website:

Password: PIN:

Email: Phone:

Security Question/Notes:

Name: ___________________________ Date: ___________

Website: _______________________________________

Password: __________________________ PIN: _______

Email: _____________________ Phone: _____________

Security Question/Notes: _______________________

____

Name: ___________________________ Date: ___________

Website: _______________________________________

Password: __________________________ PIN: _______

Email: _____________________ Phone: _____________

Security Question/Notes: _______________________

____

Name: ___________________________ Date: ___________

Website: _______________________________________

Password: __________________________ PIN: _______

Email: _____________________ Phone: _____________

Security Question/Notes: _______________________

____

Name: Date:

Website:

Password: PIN:

Email: Phone:

Security Question/Notes:

Name: Date:

Website:

Password: PIN:

Email: Phone:

Security Question/Notes:

Name: Date:

Website:

Password: PIN:

Email: Phone:

Security Question/Notes:

Name: Date:

Website:

Password: PIN:

Email: Phone:

Security Question/Notes:

Name: Date:

Website:

Password: PIN:

Email: Phone:

Security Question/Notes:

Name: Date:

Website:

Password: PIN:

Email: Phone:

Security Question/Notes:

Name: ___________________________ Date: _______________

Website: ____

Password: _____________________ PIN: _____________

Email: _________________ Phone: _________________

Security Question/Notes: _________________________

____

Name: ___________________________ Date: _______________

Website: ____

Password: _____________________ PIN: _____________

Email: _________________ Phone: _________________

Security Question/Notes: _________________________

____

Name: ___________________________ Date: _______________

Website: ____

Password: _____________________ PIN: _____________

Email: _________________ Phone: _________________

Security Question/Notes: _________________________

____

Name: Date:

Website:

Password: PIN:

Email: Phone:

Security Question/Notes:

Name: Date:

Website:

Password: PIN:

Email: Phone:

Security Question/Notes:

Name: Date:

Website:

Password: PIN:

Email: Phone:

Security Question/Notes:

Name: ___________________________ Date: ___________

Website: ____

Password: _____________________________ PIN: ________

Email: ___________________________ Phone: __________

Security Question/Notes: ___________________________

____

Name: ___________________________ Date: ___________

Website: ____

Password: _____________________________ PIN: ________

Email: ___________________________ Phone: __________

Security Question/Notes: ___________________________

____

Name: ___________________________ Date: ___________

Website: ____

Password: _____________________________ PIN: ________

Email: ___________________________ Phone: __________

Security Question/Notes: ___________________________

____

Name: ______________________ Date: ______________

Website: ____

Password: __________________________ PIN: _________

Email: ___________________ Phone: ______________

Security Question/Notes: _________________________

____

Name: ______________________ Date: ______________

Website: ____

Password: __________________________ PIN: _________

Email: ___________________ Phone: ______________

Security Question/Notes: _________________________

____

Name: ______________________ Date: ______________

Website: ____

Password: __________________________ PIN: _________

Email: ___________________ Phone: ______________

Security Question/Notes: _________________________

____

Name: ______________________ Date: __________

Website: ______________________________

Password: __________________ PIN: ________

Email: ___________________ Phone: ________

Security Question/Notes: _______________

____

Name: ______________________ Date: __________

Website: ______________________________

Password: __________________ PIN: ________

Email: ___________________ Phone: ________

Security Question/Notes: _______________

____

Name: ______________________ Date: __________

Website: ______________________________

Password: __________________ PIN: ________

Email: ___________________ Phone: ________

Security Question/Notes: _______________

____

Name: Date:

Website:

Password: PIN:

Email: Phone:

Security Question/Notes:

Name: Date:

Website:

Password: PIN:

Email: Phone:

Security Question/Notes:

Name: Date:

Website:

Password: PIN:

Email: Phone:

Security Question/Notes:

Name: _______________________ Date: _______

Website: _________________________________

Password: _______________ PIN: __________

Email: ______________ Phone: ____________

Security Question/Notes: _________________

____

Name: _______________________ Date: _______

Website: _________________________________

Password: _______________ PIN: __________

Email: ______________ Phone: ____________

Security Question/Notes: _________________

____

Name: _______________________ Date: _______

Website: _________________________________

Password: _______________ PIN: __________

Email: ______________ Phone: ____________

Security Question/Notes: _________________

____

Name: Date:

Website:

Password: PIN:

Email: Phone:

Security Question/Notes:

Name: Date:

Website:

Password: PIN:

Email: Phone:

Security Question/Notes:

Name: Date:

Website:

Password: PIN:

Email: Phone:

Security Question/Notes:

Name: Date:

Website:

Password: PIN:

Email: Phone:

Security Question/Notes:

Name: Date:

Website:

Password: PIN:

Email: Phone:

Security Question/Notes:

Name: Date:

Website:

Password: PIN:

Email: Phone:

Security Question/Notes:

Name: Date:

Website:

Password: PIN:

Email: Phone:

Security Question/Notes:

Name: Date:

Website:

Password: PIN:

Email: Phone:

Security Question/Notes:

Name: Date:

Website:

Password: PIN:

Email: Phone:

Security Question/Notes:

Name: Date:

Website:

Password: PIN:

Email: Phone:

Security Question/Notes:

Name: Date:

Website:

Password: PIN:

Email: Phone:

Security Question/Notes:

Name: Date:

Website:

Password: PIN:

Email: Phone:

Security Question/Notes:

Name: Date:

Website:

Password: PIN:

Email: Phone:

Security Question/Notes:

Name: Date:

Website:

Password: PIN:

Email: Phone:

Security Question/Notes:

Name: Date:

Website:

Password: PIN:

Email: Phone:

Security Question/Notes:

Name: _______________________ Date: _______________

Website: ____

Password: ___________________________ PIN: ___________

Email: _______________________ Phone: _______________

Security Question/Notes: ______________________________

____

Name: _______________________ Date: _______________

Website: ____

Password: ___________________________ PIN: ___________

Email: _______________________ Phone: _______________

Security Question/Notes: ______________________________

____

Name: _______________________ Date: _______________

Website: ____

Password: ___________________________ PIN: ___________

Email: _______________________ Phone: _______________

Security Question/Notes: ______________________________

____

Name: _____________________________ Date: _______________

Website: ____

Password: ______________________________ PIN: __________

Email: ______________________ Phone: __________________

Security Question/Notes: _________________________________

____

Name: _____________________________ Date: _______________

Website: ____

Password: ______________________________ PIN: __________

Email: ______________________ Phone: __________________

Security Question/Notes: _________________________________

____

Name: _____________________________ Date: _______________

Website: ____

Password: ______________________________ PIN: __________

Email: ______________________ Phone: __________________

Security Question/Notes: _________________________________

Name: Date:

Website:

Password: PIN:

Email: Phone:

Security Question/Notes:

Name: Date:

Website:

Password: PIN:

Email: Phone:

Security Question/Notes:

Name: Date:

Website:

Password: PIN:

Email: Phone:

Security Question/Notes:

Name: _______________________ Date: _______________

Website: ____

Password: _____________________ PIN: _____________

Email: ________________________ Phone: ___________

Security Question/Notes: _________________________

____

Name: _______________________ Date: _______________

Website: ____

Password: _____________________ PIN: _____________

Email: ________________________ Phone: ___________

Security Question/Notes: _________________________

____

Name: _______________________ Date: _______________

Website: ____

Password: _____________________ PIN: _____________

Email: ________________________ Phone: ___________

Security Question/Notes: _________________________

____

Name: Date:

Website:

Password: PIN:

Email: Phone:

Security Question/Notes:

Name: Date:

Website:

Password: PIN:

Email: Phone:

Security Question/Notes:

Name: Date:

Website:

Password: PIN:

Email: Phone:

Security Question/Notes:

Name: Date:

Website:

Password: PIN:

Email: Phone:

Security Question/Notes:

___

Name: Date:

Website:

Password: PIN:

Email: Phone:

Security Question/Notes:

___

Name: Date:

Website:

Password: PIN:

Email: Phone:

Security Question/Notes:

Name: Date:

Website:

Password: PIN:

Email: Phone:

Security Question/Notes:

___

Name: Date:

Website:

Password: PIN:

Email: Phone:

Security Question/Notes:

___

Name: Date:

Website:

Password: PIN:

Email: Phone:

Security Question/Notes:

Name: _______________________ Date: _______________

Website: _______________________________________

Password: __________________________ PIN: _______

Email: ___________________ Phone: ______________

Security Question/Notes: ________________________

____

Name: _______________________ Date: _______________

Website: _______________________________________

Password: __________________________ PIN: _______

Email: ___________________ Phone: ______________

Security Question/Notes: ________________________

____

Name: _______________________ Date: _______________

Website: _______________________________________

Password: __________________________ PIN: _______

Email: ___________________ Phone: ______________

Security Question/Notes: ________________________

____

K-L

Name: ______________________ Date: ______________

Website: ____

Password: __________________________ PIN: __________

Email: ____________________ Phone: ________________

Security Question/Notes: ____________________________

____

Name: ______________________ Date: ______________

Website: ____

Password: __________________________ PIN: __________

Email: ____________________ Phone: ________________

Security Question/Notes: ____________________________

____

Name: ______________________ Date: ______________

Website: ____

Password: __________________________ PIN: __________

Email: ____________________ Phone: ________________

Security Question/Notes: ____________________________

____

Name: Date:

Website:

Password: PIN:

Email: Phone:

Security Question/Notes:

Name: Date:

Website:

Password: PIN:

Email: Phone:

Security Question/Notes:

Name: Date:

Website:

Password: PIN:

Email: Phone:

Security Question/Notes:

Name: Date:

Website:

Password: PIN:

Email: Phone:

Security Question/Notes:

Name: Date:

Website:

Password: PIN:

Email: Phone:

Security Question/Notes:

Name: Date:

Website:

Password: PIN:

Email: Phone:

Security Question/Notes:

Name: Date:

Website:

Password: PIN:

Email: Phone:

Security Question/Notes:

Name: Date:

Website:

Password: PIN:

Email: Phone:

Security Question/Notes:

Name: Date:

Website:

Password: PIN:

Email: Phone:

Security Question/Notes:

Name: Date:

Website:

Password: PIN:

Email: Phone:

Security Question/Notes:

Name: Date:

Website:

Password: PIN:

Email: Phone:

Security Question/Notes:

Name: Date:

Website:

Password: PIN:

Email: Phone:

Security Question/Notes:

Name: _______________________ Date: _______________

Website: ____

Password: _______________________ PIN: __________

Email: _______________________ Phone: __________

Security Question/Notes: ________________________

____

Name: _______________________ Date: _______________

Website: ____

Password: _______________________ PIN: __________

Email: _______________________ Phone: __________

Security Question/Notes: ________________________

____

Name: _______________________ Date: _______________

Website: ____

Password: _______________________ PIN: __________

Email: _______________________ Phone: __________

Security Question/Notes: ________________________

____

Name: Date:

Website:

Password: PIN:

Email: Phone:

Security Question/Notes:

Name: Date:

Website:

Password: PIN:

Email: Phone:

Security Question/Notes:

Name: Date:

Website:

Password: PIN:

Email: Phone:

Security Question/Notes:

Name: ______________________________ Date: ______________

Website: ____

Password: _______________________________ PIN: ___________

Email: _________________________ Phone: _________________

Security Question/Notes: _________________________________

____

Name: ______________________________ Date: ______________

Website: ____

Password: _______________________________ PIN: ___________

Email: _________________________ Phone: _________________

Security Question/Notes: _________________________________

____

Name: ______________________________ Date: ______________

Website: ____

Password: _______________________________ PIN: ___________

Email: _________________________ Phone: _________________

Security Question/Notes: _________________________________

____

Name: Date:

Website:

Password: PIN:

Email: Phone:

Security Question/Notes:

Name: Date:

Website:

Password: PIN:

Email: Phone:

Security Question/Notes:

Name: Date:

Website:

Password: PIN:

Email: Phone:

Security Question/Notes:

Name: Date:

Website:

Password: PIN:

Email: Phone:

Security Question/Notes:

Name: Date:

Website:

Password: PIN:

Email: Phone:

Security Question/Notes:

Name: Date:

Website:

Password: PIN:

Email: Phone:

Security Question/Notes:

Name: Date:

Website:

Password: PIN:

Email: Phone:

Security Question/Notes:

Name: Date:

Website:

Password: PIN:

Email: Phone:

Security Question/Notes:

Name: Date:

Website:

Password: PIN:

Email: Phone:

Security Question/Notes:

Name: Date:

Website:

Password: PIN:

Email: Phone:

Security Question/Notes:

Name: Date:

Website:

Password: PIN:

Email: Phone:

Security Question/Notes:

Name: Date:

Website:

Password: PIN:

Email: Phone:

Security Question/Notes:

Name: Date:

Website:

Password: PIN:

Email: Phone:

Security Question/Notes:

Name: Date:

Website:

Password: PIN:

Email: Phone:

Security Question/Notes:

Name: Date:

Website:

Password: PIN:

Email: Phone:

Security Question/Notes:

Name: ______________________________ Date: ______________

Website: ____

Password: ____________________________ PIN: ____________

Email: ______________________ Phone: ________________

Security Question/Notes: ______________________________

____

Name: ______________________________ Date: ______________

Website: ____

Password: ____________________________ PIN: ____________

Email: ______________________ Phone: ________________

Security Question/Notes: ______________________________

____

Name: ______________________________ Date: ______________

Website: ____

Password: ____________________________ PIN: ____________

Email: ______________________ Phone: ________________

Security Question/Notes: ______________________________

____

Name: ___________________________ Date: _______________

Website: ____

Password: ______________________________ PIN: __________

Email: ________________________ Phone: ________________

Security Question/Notes: _________________________________

____

Name: ___________________________ Date: _______________

Website: ____

Password: ______________________________ PIN: __________

Email: ________________________ Phone: ________________

Security Question/Notes: _________________________________

____

Name: ___________________________ Date: _______________

Website: ____

Password: ______________________________ PIN: __________

Email: ________________________ Phone: ________________

Security Question/Notes: _________________________________

____

Name: Date:

Website:

Password: PIN:

Email: Phone:

Security Question/Notes:

Name: Date:

Website:

Password: PIN:

Email: Phone:

Security Question/Notes:

Name: Date:

Website:

Password: PIN:

Email: Phone:

Security Question/Notes:

Name: ___________________________ Date: ___________

Website: ____

Password: _______________________ PIN: ___________

Email: _________________________ Phone: __________

Security Question/Notes: _________________________

____

Name: ___________________________ Date: ___________

Website: ____

Password: _______________________ PIN: ___________

Email: _________________________ Phone: __________

Security Question/Notes: _________________________

____

Name: ___________________________ Date: ___________

Website: ____

Password: _______________________ PIN: ___________

Email: _________________________ Phone: __________

Security Question/Notes: _________________________

____

Name: Date:

Website:

Password: PIN:

Email: Phone:

Security Question/Notes:

Name: Date:

Website:

Password: PIN:

Email: Phone:

Security Question/Notes:

Name: Date:

Website:

Password: PIN:

Email: Phone:

Security Question/Notes:

Name: ____________________ Date: ____________________

Website: ____________________

Password: ____________________ PIN: ____________________

Email: ____________________ Phone: ____________________

Security Question/Notes: ____________________

____

Name: ____________________ Date: ____________________

Website: ____________________

Password: ____________________ PIN: ____________________

Email: ____________________ Phone: ____________________

Security Question/Notes: ____________________

____

Name: ____________________ Date: ____________________

Website: ____________________

Password: ____________________ PIN: ____________________

Email: ____________________ Phone: ____________________

Security Question/Notes: ____________________

____

Name: ___________________________ Date: _______________

Website: ____

Password: ____________________________ PIN: _____________

Email: ______________________ Phone: __________________

Security Question/Notes: _________________________________

____

Name: ___________________________ Date: _______________

Website: ____

Password: ____________________________ PIN: _____________

Email: ______________________ Phone: __________________

Security Question/Notes: _________________________________

____

Name: ___________________________ Date: _______________

Website: ____

Password: ____________________________ PIN: _____________

Email: ______________________ Phone: __________________

Security Question/Notes: _________________________________

____

Name: Date:

Website:

Password: PIN:

Email: Phone:

Security Question/Notes:

Name: Date:

Website:

Password: PIN:

Email: Phone:

Security Question/Notes:

Name: Date:

Website:

Password: PIN:

Email: Phone:

Security Question/Notes:

Name: Date:

Website:

Password: PIN:

Email: Phone:

Security Question/Notes:

Name: Date:

Website:

Password: PIN:

Email: Phone:

Security Question/Notes:

Name: Date:

Website:

Password: PIN:

Email: Phone:

Security Question/Notes:

Name: _______________________ Date: _______

Website: _________________________________

Password: ___________________ PIN: _______

Email: ____________________ Phone: _______

Security Question/Notes: _________________

____

Name: _______________________ Date: _______

Website: _________________________________

Password: ___________________ PIN: _______

Email: ____________________ Phone: _______

Security Question/Notes: _________________

____

Name: _______________________ Date: _______

Website: _________________________________

Password: ___________________ PIN: _______

Email: ____________________ Phone: _______

Security Question/Notes: _________________

____

Name: Date:

Website:

Password: PIN:

Email: Phone:

Security Question/Notes:

Name: Date:

Website:

Password: PIN:

Email: Phone:

Security Question/Notes:

Name: Date:

Website:

Password: PIN:

Email: Phone:

Security Question/Notes:

Name: ___________________________ Date: ___________

Website: ____

Password: _____________________ PIN: ____________

Email: ________________ Phone: __________________

Security Question/Notes: _________________________

____

Name: ___________________________ Date: ___________

Website: ____

Password: _____________________ PIN: ____________

Email: ________________ Phone: __________________

Security Question/Notes: _________________________

____

Name: ___________________________ Date: ___________

Website: ____

Password: _____________________ PIN: ____________

Email: ________________ Phone: __________________

Security Question/Notes: _________________________

____

Name: Date:

Website:

Password: PIN:

Email: Phone:

Security Question/Notes:

Name: Date:

Website:

Password: PIN:

Email: Phone:

Security Question/Notes:

Name: Date:

Website:

Password: PIN:

Email: Phone:

Security Question/Notes:

Name: Date:

Website:

Password: PIN:

Email: Phone:

Security Question/Notes:

Name: Date:

Website:

Password: PIN:

Email: Phone:

Security Question/Notes:

Name: Date:

Website:

Password: PIN:

Email: Phone:

Security Question/Notes:

Name: ___________________________ Date: _______

Website: _________________________

Password: ________________________ PIN: _______

Email: ___________________ Phone: __________

Security Question/Notes: ___________________

____

Name: ___________________________ Date: _______

Website: _________________________

Password: ________________________ PIN: _______

Email: ___________________ Phone: __________

Security Question/Notes: ___________________

____

Name: ___________________________ Date: _______

Website: _________________________

Password: ________________________ PIN: _______

Email: ___________________ Phone: __________

Security Question/Notes: ___________________

____

Name: Date:

Website:

Password: PIN:

Email: Phone:

Security Question/Notes:

Name: Date:

Website:

Password: PIN:

Email: Phone:

Security Question/Notes:

Name: Date:

Website:

Password: PIN:

Email: Phone:

Security Question/Notes:

Name: Date:

Website:

Password: PIN:

Email: Phone:

Security Question/Notes:

Name: Date:

Website:

Password: PIN:

Email: Phone:

Security Question/Notes:

Name: Date:

Website:

Password: PIN:

Email: Phone:

Security Question/Notes:

Name: ________________________ Date: ______________

Website: ______________________________________

Password: ____________________ PIN: ____________

Email: ______________________ Phone: __________

Security Question/Notes: ________________________

____

Name: ________________________ Date: ______________

Website: ______________________________________

Password: ____________________ PIN: ____________

Email: ______________________ Phone: __________

Security Question/Notes: ________________________

____

Name: ________________________ Date: ______________

Website: ______________________________________

Password: ____________________ PIN: ____________

Email: ______________________ Phone: __________

Security Question/Notes: ________________________

____

Name: Date:

Website:

Password: PIN:

Email: Phone:

Security Question/Notes:

Name: Date:

Website:

Password: PIN:

Email: Phone:

Security Question/Notes:

Name: Date:

Website:

Password: PIN:

Email: Phone:

Security Question/Notes:

Name: _______________ Date: _______________

Website: _______________

Password: _______________ PIN: _______________

Email: _______________ Phone: _______________

Security Question/Notes: _______________

____

Name: _______________ Date: _______________

Website: _______________

Password: _______________ PIN: _______________

Email: _______________ Phone: _______________

Security Question/Notes: _______________

____

Name: _______________ Date: _______________

Website: _______________

Password: _______________ PIN: _______________

Email: _______________ Phone: _______________

Security Question/Notes: _______________

____

Name: Date:

Website:

Password: PIN:

Email: Phone:

Security Question/Notes:

Name: Date:

Website:

Password: PIN:

Email: Phone:

Security Question/Notes:

Name: Date:

Website:

Password: PIN:

Email: Phone:

Security Question/Notes:

Name: Date:

Website:

Password: PIN:

Email: Phone:

Security Question/Notes:

Name: Date:

Website:

Password: PIN:

Email: Phone:

Security Question/Notes:

Name: Date:

Website:

Password: PIN:

Email: Phone:

Security Question/Notes:

Name: Date:

Website:

Password: PIN:

Email: Phone:

Security Question/Notes:

Name: Date:

Website:

Password: PIN:

Email: Phone:

Security Question/Notes:

Name: Date:

Website:

Password: PIN:

Email: Phone:

Security Question/Notes:

Name: Date:

Website:

Password: PIN:

Email: Phone:

Security Question/Notes:

Name: Date:

Website:

Password: PIN:

Email: Phone:

Security Question/Notes:

Name: Date:

Website:

Password: PIN:

Email: Phone:

Security Question/Notes:

Name: Date:

Website:

Password: PIN:

Email: Phone:

Security Question/Notes:

Name: Date:

Website:

Password: PIN:

Email: Phone:

Security Question/Notes:

Name: Date:

Website:

Password: PIN:

Email: Phone:

Security Question/Notes:

Name: Date:

Website:

Password: PIN:

Email: Phone:

Security Question/Notes:

Name: Date:

Website:

Password: PIN:

Email: Phone:

Security Question/Notes:

Name: Date:

Website:

Password: PIN:

Email: Phone:

Security Question/Notes:

Name: Date:

Website:

Password: PIN:

Email: Phone:

Security Question/Notes:

Name: Date:

Website:

Password: PIN:

Email: Phone:

Security Question/Notes:

Name: Date:

Website:

Password: PIN:

Email: Phone:

Security Question/Notes:

Name: _______________________ Date: _______________

Website: ____

Password: ___________________________ PIN: __________

Email: _______________________ Phone: ______________

Security Question/Notes: _____________________________

____

Name: ________________________ Date: ______________

Website: ____

Password: ___________________________ PIN: __________

Email: _______________________ Phone: ______________

Security Question/Notes: _____________________________

____

Name: ________________________ Date: ______________

Website: ____

Password: ___________________________ PIN: __________

Email: _______________________ Phone: ______________

Security Question/Notes: _____________________________

____

Name: ___________________________ Date: ___________

Website: ____

Password: _____________________ PIN: ___________

Email: ________________ Phone: __________________

Security Question/Notes: _________________________

____

Name: ___________________________ Date: ___________

Website: ____

Password: _____________________ PIN: ___________

Email: ________________ Phone: __________________

Security Question/Notes: _________________________

____

Name: ___________________________ Date: ___________

Website: ____

Password: _____________________ PIN: ___________

Email: ________________ Phone: __________________

Security Question/Notes: _________________________

____

Name: Date:

Website:

Password: PIN:

Email: Phone:

Security Question/Notes:

Name: Date:

Website:

Password: PIN:

Email: Phone:

Security Question/Notes:

Name: Date:

Website:

Password: PIN:

Email: Phone:

Security Question/Notes:

Name: ___________________________ Date: ___________

Website: ____

Password: _______________________ PIN: ___________

Email: __________________________ Phone: _________

Security Question/Notes: _________________________

____

Name: ___________________________ Date: ___________

Website: ____

Password: _______________________ PIN: ___________

Email: __________________________ Phone: _________

Security Question/Notes: _________________________

____

Name: ___________________________ Date: ___________

Website: ____

Password: _______________________ PIN: ___________

Email: __________________________ Phone: _________

Security Question/Notes: _________________________

____

Name: _______________________ Date: _______________

Website: ____

Password: _____________________ PIN: _____________

Email: ________________________ Phone: ___________

Security Question/Notes: _________________________

____

Name: _______________________ Date: _______________

Website: ____

Password: _____________________ PIN: _____________

Email: ________________________ Phone: ___________

Security Question/Notes: _________________________

____

Name: _______________________ Date: _______________

Website: ____

Password: _____________________ PIN: _____________

Email: ________________________ Phone: ___________

Security Question/Notes: _________________________

____

Name: Date:

Website:

Password: PIN:

Email: Phone:

Security Question/Notes:

Name: Date:

Website:

Password: PIN:

Email: Phone:

Security Question/Notes:

Name: Date:

Website:

Password: PIN:

Email: Phone:

Security Question/Notes:

Name: _______________________ Date: _______________________

Website: ____

Password: ____________________ PIN: ________________

Email: _______________________ Phone: ______________

Security Question/Notes: _____________________________

____

Name: _______________________ Date: _______________________

Website: ____

Password: ____________________ PIN: ________________

Email: _______________________ Phone: ______________

Security Question/Notes: _____________________________

____

Name: _______________________ Date: _______________________

Website: ____

Password: ____________________ PIN: ________________

Email: _______________________ Phone: ______________

Security Question/Notes: _____________________________

____

Name: Date:

Website:

Password: PIN:

Email: Phone:

Security Question/Notes:

Name: Date:

Website:

Password: PIN:

Email: Phone:

Security Question/Notes:

Name: Date:

Website:

Password: PIN:

Email: Phone:

Security Question/Notes:

Name: _______________________ Date: _______________

Website: ____

Password: _______________________ PIN: _____________

Email: ______________________ Phone: ________________

Security Question/Notes: _____________________________

____

Name: _______________________ Date: _______________

Website: ____

Password: _______________________ PIN: _____________

Email: ______________________ Phone: ________________

Security Question/Notes: _____________________________

____

Name: _______________________ Date: _______________

Website: ____

Password: _______________________ PIN: _____________

Email: ______________________ Phone: ________________

Security Question/Notes: _____________________________

____

Name: _______________________ Date: _______

Website: _______________________

Password: _______________ PIN: _______

Email: _______________ Phone: _______

Security Question/Notes: _______________

____

Name: _______________________ Date: _______

Website: _______________________

Password: _______________ PIN: _______

Email: _______________ Phone: _______

Security Question/Notes: _______________

____

Name: _______________________ Date: _______

Website: _______________________

Password: _______________ PIN: _______

Email: _______________ Phone: _______

Security Question/Notes: _______________

____

Name: Date:

Website:

Password: PIN:

Email: Phone:

Security Question/Notes:

Name: Date:

Website:

Password: PIN:

Email: Phone:

Security Question/Notes:

Name: Date:

Website:

Password: PIN:

Email: Phone:

Security Question/Notes:

Name: Date:

Website:

Password: PIN:

Email: Phone:

Security Question/Notes:

Name: Date:

Website:

Password: PIN:

Email: Phone:

Security Question/Notes:

Name: Date:

Website:

Password: PIN:

Email: Phone:

Security Question/Notes:

Name: _______________________ Date: _______________

Website: _____________________________________

Password: _________________________ PIN: _______

Email: _____________________ Phone: ___________

Security Question/Notes: _____________________

____

Name: _______________________ Date: _______________

Website: _____________________________________

Password: _________________________ PIN: _______

Email: _____________________ Phone: ___________

Security Question/Notes: _____________________

____

Name: _______________________ Date: _______________

Website: _____________________________________

Password: _________________________ PIN: _______

Email: _____________________ Phone: ___________

Security Question/Notes: _____________________

____

Name: ___________________________ Date: ___________

Website: ___________________________________

Password: _________________________ PIN: ________

Email: _____________________ Phone: ___________

Security Question/Notes: ___________________________

____

Name: ___________________________ Date: ___________

Website: ___________________________________

Password: _________________________ PIN: ________

Email: _____________________ Phone: ___________

Security Question/Notes: ___________________________

____

Name: ___________________________ Date: ___________

Website: ___________________________________

Password: _________________________ PIN: ________

Email: _____________________ Phone: ___________

Security Question/Notes: ___________________________

____

Name: Date:

Website:

Password: PIN:

Email: Phone:

Security Question/Notes:

Name: Date:

Website:

Password: PIN:

Email: Phone:

Security Question/Notes:

Name: Date:

Website:

Password: PIN:

Email: Phone:

Security Question/Notes:

Name:

Date:

Website:

Password:

PIN:

Email:

Phone:

Security Question/Notes:

Name:

Date:

Website:

Password:

PIN:

Email:

Phone:

Security Question/Notes:

Name:

Date:

Website:

Password:

PIN:

Email:

Phone:

Security Question/Notes:

Name: ___________________________ Date: ___________

Website: ____

Password: _______________________ PIN: ______________

Email: ___________________ Phone: _________________

Security Question/Notes: _____________________________

____

Name: _______________________________ Date: _________

Website: ____

Password: _______________________ PIN: ______________

Email: ___________________ Phone: _________________

Security Question/Notes: _____________________________

____

Name: _______________________________ Date: _________

Website: ____

Password: _______________________ PIN: ______________

Email: ___________________ Phone: _________________

Security Question/Notes: _____________________________

____

Name: _____________________ Date: _______

Website: _____________________

Password: _____________________ PIN: _______

Email: _____________________ Phone: _______

Security Question/Notes: _____________________

____

Name: _____________________ Date: _______

Website: _____________________

Password: _____________________ PIN: _______

Email: _____________________ Phone: _______

Security Question/Notes: _____________________

____

Name: _____________________ Date: _______

Website: _____________________

Password: _____________________ PIN: _______

Email: _____________________ Phone: _______

Security Question/Notes: _____________________

____

NOTE   PAGE

NOTE   PAGE

NOTE

PAGE

Made in the USA
Monee, IL
07 July 2026

56553295R00069